The ROCK CYCLE

Wendy Conklin

Consultant

Jill Tobin
California Teacher of the Year
Semi-Finalist
Burbank Unified School District

Publishing Credits

Rachelle Cracchiolo, M.S.Ed., *Publisher*
Conni Medina, M.A.Ed., *Managing Editor*
Diana Kenney, M.A.Ed., NBCT, *Senior Editor*
Dona Herweck Rice, *Series Developer*
Robin Erickson, *Multimedia Designer*
Timothy Bradley, *Illustrator*

Image Credits: Cover, p.1 4FR/iStock; p.19 Dirk Wiersma / Science Source; p.10 Francois Gohier / Science Source; pp.2, 4, 6, 7, 9, 11, 12, 13, 14, 17, 18, 19, 20, 21, 25, 26, 30, 31, 32 iStock; p.28, 29 Janelle Bell-Martin; p.17 John Valley, University of Wisconsin- Madison; p.13 Joyce Photographics / Science Source; p.23 Martin Shields / Science Source; p.11 NOAA Ocean Explorer, USGS; p.17 Spencer Sutton / Science Source; all other images from Shutterstock.

Library of Congress Cataloging-in-Publication Data

Conklin, Wendy, author.
  The rock cycle / Wendy Conklin.
    pages cm
  Summary: "Rocks may not look like they are doing much. But they are always forming, destructing, and recycling. Different types of rocks form in different ways. And different types of rocks have a variety of uses. Take a journey through the rock cycle and stand in rock-solid awe of our planet"-- Provided by publisher.
  Audience: Grades 4-6.
  Includes index.
  ISBN 978-1-4807-4688-6 (pbk.) -- ISBN 1-4807-4688-6 (pbk.)
1. Petrology--Juvenile literature. 2. Geochemical cycles--Juvenile literature. I. Title.
  QE432.2.C66 2016
  552--dc23
                                                   2014045211

Teacher Created Materials

5301 Oceanus Drive
Huntington Beach, CA 92649-1030
http://www.tcmpub.com
ISBN 978-1-4807-4688-6
© 2016 Teacher Created Materials, Inc.

Table of Contents

A Long Journey

Have you ever had the urge to change into something else? It can be hard for humans, but rocks do it all the time! Rocks? The same rocks that look like they're just sitting there doing nothing? Yes! Rocks are constantly on the move, but the movement is so slow that it's hard for us to see. But if you could keep your eyes open for a couple million years, you could watch a mountain turn into sand!

These drastic changes in rocks are part of the rock cycle. A cycle is a set of repeating patterns. In the rock cycle, rocks constantly form, destruct, and recycle.

There are three basic types of rock: sedimentary, metamorphic, and igneous. Over time, one type of rock can change into another. Rocks change through **weathering**, heat, pressure, and **erosion**. Rock on!

Introducing Igneous Rock!

How exciting would it be to see a volcano blasting hot lava from its center! But did you ever wonder where this hot lava comes from and what makes it rise to the surface? And what does this have to do with the rock cycle?

It's amazing to think of Earth as one gigantic rock. Earth's outer layer is known as the *crust*. Underneath Earth's crust lies the mantle. This is a layer of extremely hot rock. Rocks that rise from the mantle melt because of the intense heat found there. This melting rock forms **magma**. Some magma stays underground. But when magma pushes up to Earth's surface, a volcano erupts.

Magma that reaches Earth's surface is called *lava*. Air causes lava to cool and harden. Finally, igneous rocks form. While it can take millions of years for other types of rock to form, some igneous rocks can take just a few hours! But why does magma rise to Earth's surface?

Volcanic Rock

The least **dense** rock on Earth is called *pumice*. Pumice is formed when lava cools quickly and air bubbles form. With so much air, the rock is less dense than water, and it can float.

Extrusive or Intrusive

There are two types of igneous rocks: extrusive and intrusive. Extrusive igneous rocks are produced aboveground when lava hardens after a volcanic eruption. Intrusive igneous rocks are produced when magma slowly cools underground.

Pumice is used in products people use every day such as makeup and toothpaste.

Breaking Up Is Hard to Do

Earth's crust is broken into many large pieces called **tectonic plates**. Plate boundaries are where the plates meet. It's at these boundaries that many igneous rocks form. Some plates move apart while other plates move toward each other. This movement does not happen overnight. Instead, it takes years and years to notice this movement.

When plates move apart, something has to fill the gaps. This is where magma from the mantle rises and melts. The magma forms new crust in these gaps. It cools and produces igneous rock.

When plates move towards each other, sometimes one plate sinks into the mantle, allowing the other plate to rise. The plate that sinks melts from the heat and forms new magma.

The Mid-Atlantic Ridge is the meeting place of tectonic plates and can be seen in Iceland before it disappears again into the Atlantic Ocean.

Mid-Atlantic Ridge

When tectonic plates slide past each other, the earth quakes.

Pangaea

Hundreds of thousands of years ago, all the continents were connected. They formed one giant super-continent called *Pangaea*. The tectonic plates slowly moved and drifted apart. A water body called the *Tethys Sea* helped split Pangaea in two.

Hot Spots

At times, magma finds its way to Earth's crust through hot spots. Hot spots are exactly what they sound like: areas where the temperature is extremely high under Earth's tectonic plates.

Igneous Rocks Are So Cool

If you were searching for igneous rocks, where would you look? Near a volcano would be a good choice. Here, the tectonic plates move toward one another. Volcanoes form at these places. When lava flows, it cools and hardens into igneous rock. If lava blasts into the sky, it may cool and harden while still in the air. When this happens, it is called a **volcanic bomb**. Think of it like a bottle of soda. If you shake the bottle, the gases separate from the liquid and bubbles form. When you take off the cap, it explodes! Similarly, gases in magma break apart when it erupts. Volcanic rock and ash are sent flying into the air. Over time, igneous rocks will also form from the layers of ashes.

Igneous rocks make up 95 percent of Earth's crust, mountains, and even the moon!

volcanic bomb

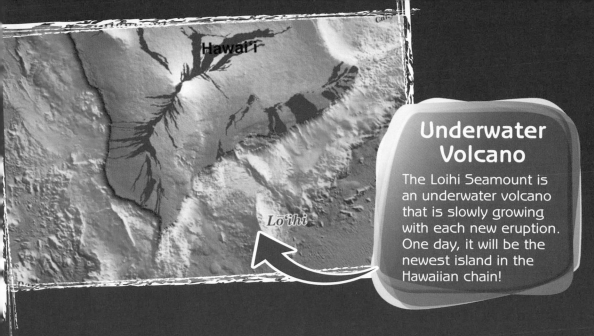

Hawai'i

Loʻihi

Another good place to look for igneous rocks is underground. Some magma doesn't make its way through the crust. Instead, it cools near the crust, and rocks form under the surface.

Under the ocean is where you will find the most igneous rock. Igneous rocks can form when plates move apart. This plate movement often takes place on the ocean floor. Lava reaches the water and cools, making igneous rocks.

Igneous rocks can change over time. Wind, rain, snow, and ice wear rocks down into tiny pieces. Sedimentary rocks form from this weathering. And if igneous rocks get hot and are under enough pressure, they turn into metamorphic rocks.

Granite is one example of igneous rock. Granite is often used to make kitchen countertops.

Meet Metamorphic Rock!

Take a close look at the word *metamorphic*. You will notice that it looks a lot like the word *metamorphosis*. The two words are very similar, and both have to do with change. When a butterfly undergoes metamorphosis, it changes from a caterpillar into a butterfly. When rocks undergo **metamorphism**, they change to new types of rock. In order for this to happen, the rocks must be exposed to heat, pressure, or both.

Metamorphic rocks are part of the rock cycle. If you look for metamorphic rocks, you will need to do some digging. You will most likely find metamorphic rocks underneath Earth's surface. These changes can take millions of years. But how does the process work?

Almost all rocks are made of **minerals**. Some rocks have a mixture of minerals. Other rocks might have just one mineral. Heat and pressure break down a rock's minerals. Then, new minerals form. These minerals can often be seen in metamorphic rocks as **crystals**. When a rock changes into a new type of rock, no new materials are added or taken away. The atoms that make up the minerals are just rearranged within the rock.

amethyst crystals

Sparkle and Shine

Slate is a type of metamorphic rock. When slate forms, a mineral called *mica* sometimes replaces a portion of the clay that was in the original rock. Mica is the mineral that makes slate shine and granite sparkle.

The Heat Is On!

Metamorphic rocks are formed in two ways. The first is by heat. Indeed, rocks are hard, but they are not beyond destruction. As magma rises to the surface, it flows past rocks on its way through Earth's crust. Magma can be hotter than 1,000° Celsius (1,832° Fahrenheit). Think about what this heat could do to a rock!

Sometimes, magma pushes its way up through layers of rock. Heat from the magma destroys the minerals in the rocks. Then, crystals of new minerals form. New metamorphic rocks are born. Scientists call this *contact metamorphism*. It's called this because the magma changes the rocks as they come into contact with each other. This type of metamorphism is caused mainly by heat. But metamorphic rocks can also be formed by adding pressure.

Olivine crystals are made through contact metamorphism.

Foliated or Non-Foliated

Each type of metamorphic rock can be classified as either *foliated* or *non-foliated*. Foliation is the layering of crystals and minerals in the rock. This occurs when the rock is under pressure.

Pro Parents

The original rock that changes to form a metamorphic rock is the parent rock. Scientists have named this parent rock *protolith*.

One of the best-known metamorphic rocks is the diamond.

Under Pressure

Metamorphic rocks also form because of pressure from plate tectonics. Think about two plates moving toward each other. One plate has to give in and sink beneath the other plate. The other plate rises. During this process, the rocks underground are crushed. This creates an amazing amount of pressure. This intense pressure creates heat. Sometimes, the heat is so intense that it melts the rocks (forming igneous rocks). But other times, the heat cooks the rocks, changing their mineral structure and forming metamorphic rocks.

Earth's plates are very large. So, when rocks form from plate movement, it happens over hundreds or thousands of miles. When the process happens over this large area or region, scientists call it **regional metamorphism**.

Plate movement is why you are likely to find metamorphic rocks at the bases of mountain ranges. These are the oldest rocks on Earth. In fact, some are billions of years old!

Scientists use metamorphic rocks as a tool to study Earth. The rocks show scientists what happens under Earth's crust.

marble

Ancient Rubble

The oldest rock on Earth is a crystal that was part of a metamorphic rock. It was found in Australia and is 4.4 billion years old!

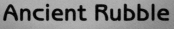

Buried Alive!

One form of metamorphism is called *burial metamorphism*. Burial metamorphism usually happens when sedimentary rocks are deeply buried. These rocks are usually not foliated or are very weakly foliated.

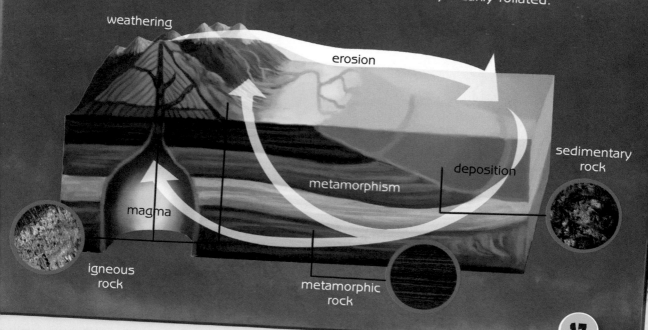

weathering

erosion

deposition

sedimentary rock

metamorphism

magma

igneous rock

metamorphic rock

Say Hello to Sedimentary Rock!

Imagine a large mountain covered in melting ice. As the ice melts, small pieces of the mountain break off. These pieces flow down the mountain and into a river. These small pieces of mountain are **sediments**. The river carries these muddy sediments to the bottom of the ocean, where they settle on the ocean floor. Other sediments pile on top in the same way. This creates intense pressure. For years and years this happens. Sediments continue to pile on top of one another, creating layers called **strata**. Over a long period of time, this process repeats itself, and new rocks are created—sedimentary rocks.

Cool Coal

When plants die in wet areas, they turn into a material called **peat**, instead of completely decaying with time. The peat is buried and compressed. And after millions of years, it becomes coal.

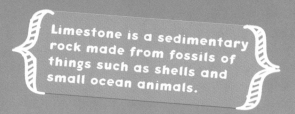
Limestone is a sedimentary rock made from fossils of things such as shells and small ocean animals.

Inside sedimentary rocks, you will find sediments. In fact, there might be millions of pieces of sediment in a rock! But you might also see tiny fossils and shells, too. These fossils and shells come from sea creatures. Some of these creatures may have lived long ago, and their skeletons formed the fossils we find today. These fossils settle on the ocean floor. Over the years, the sediments and fossils layer on top of each other. It takes a long time, but eventually, sedimentary rocks are formed.

mudstone with fossilized aquatic animals

Finding Fossils

Because of the way that sedimentary rocks are created, they are most likely to have fossils in them. Some mudstone cliffs in England have fossils from about 140 million years ago.

Weathering and Erosion

Sedimentary rocks begin with sediments. And sediments are created through weathering and erosion. Weathering is the slow breakdown of rocks. It occurs when rain, wind, or ice break up rock. Wind can blow against rocks and break them apart. Rain can wear away at a rock. It can also get into cracks of the rock. When the water freezes, the crack widens. Over time, this breaks down the rock into smaller pieces. Large changes in temperature makes rocks shrink and expand. This weakens rocks. Over time, the rocks break up into smaller pieces.

Sliding Downhill

The three most common types of erosion are water, wind, and gravity erosion. The movement of water and wind against rocks causes water and wind erosion. Gravity erosion is a bit different since it is caused by downhill movement. The most well-known occurrences of gravity erosion are landslides.

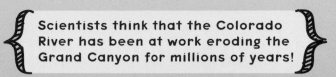

Scientists think that the Colorado River has been at work eroding the Grand Canyon for millions of years!

Erosion is the movement of weathered rock and sediment. This can occur several ways. Glaciers may break up rocks. Then, water carries the sediment to other areas. Wind and rain also carry sediments to new places. When sediments reach their destination, they are deposited. The word *deposition* comes from *deposit*. Scientists call this process *erosion and deposition*.

Weathering and erosion work together to turn rocks into sediments. Wind may blow sand at a rock, causing it to weather. Then, wind may erode the rock by blowing the sediments to another location.

This rock has an amazing resemblance to a dog's head. This was caused by weathering and erosion.

Making Sedimentary Rock

Wind, water, and ice draw sediments away from rocks. At some point, the water and wind slow down. Then, this sediment finds a resting place, and layers form. You can find these layers at the bottom of rivers. Beaches and sandbanks are ideal places for layers to form, too. In the desert, wind blows sediments into sand dunes.

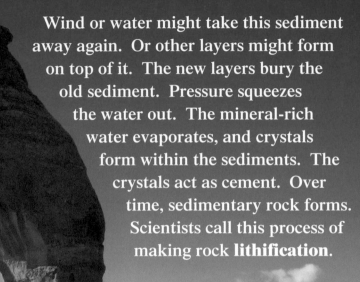

Wind or water might take this sediment away again. Or other layers might form on top of it. The new layers bury the old sediment. Pressure squeezes the water out. The mineral-rich water evaporates, and crystals form within the sediments. The crystals act as cement. Over time, sedimentary rock forms. Scientists call this process of making rock **lithification**.

Ch—Ch—Ch—Changes!

Once sediments have been deposited, sedimentary rocks go through other changes. These changes are called *diagenesis* (dahy-uh-JEN-uh-sis). Diagenesis includes the physical and chemical changes that turn sediment into sedimentary rock.

You can see layers in these types of rocks. If you look close enough, you will find that some layers have large sediment. Other layers have small sediment.

Skeletons, shells, and plants collect on the floor of the ocean. Sediments build up around these, and rocks form. It takes millions of years to form rocks this way!

If scientists find a layer of bird skeletons in sedimentary rock, they know that birds lived in that area.

conglomerate rock

Rockin' with Rocks

When you see a large rock that looks like it's made up of smaller rocks, it's called either a *conglomerate* or a *breccia* (BRECH-ee-uh). A conglomerate is made up of round rocks, and a breccia is made up of sharp, angled rocks.

Recycling Rock

The rock cycle shows how rocks are recycled. But that doesn't mean we can trace one specific rock and see how it changes into all three rocks and back again. We can, however, see how these rocks break down and form into other types of rocks. This recycling of rocks takes millions of years.

We can start at any place in the rock cycle to see how rocks change. Magma pushes through the crust and erupts in a volcano. Igneous rocks form on mountains when lava cools. Over time, wind and rain erode rocks. These small sediments wash downhill and deposit in riverbeds. Layers and layers deposit on top. With enough pressure, sedimentary rocks form. Earth's plates move and cause the rocks to be buried underground. Pressure heats up and cooks the rocks. As a result, metamorphic rocks form under Earth's crust. If magma reaches these rocks, it can melt them which can then form igneous rocks. The cycle continues over and over.

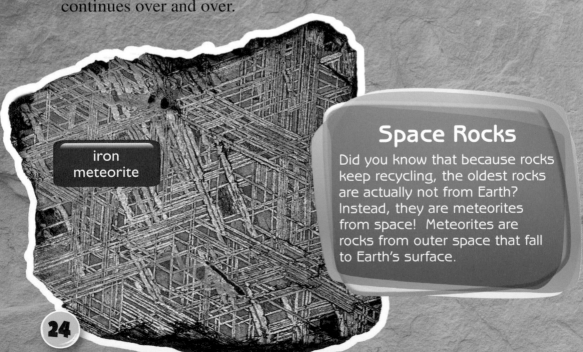

iron meteorite

Space Rocks

Did you know that because rocks keep recycling, the oldest rocks are actually not from Earth? Instead, they are meteorites from space! Meteorites are rocks from outer space that fall to Earth's surface.

Intertwined

The rock cycle is not a simple circle. Rocks can change to any type of rock at any time. Metamorphic rocks can even change into a different type of metamorphic rock.

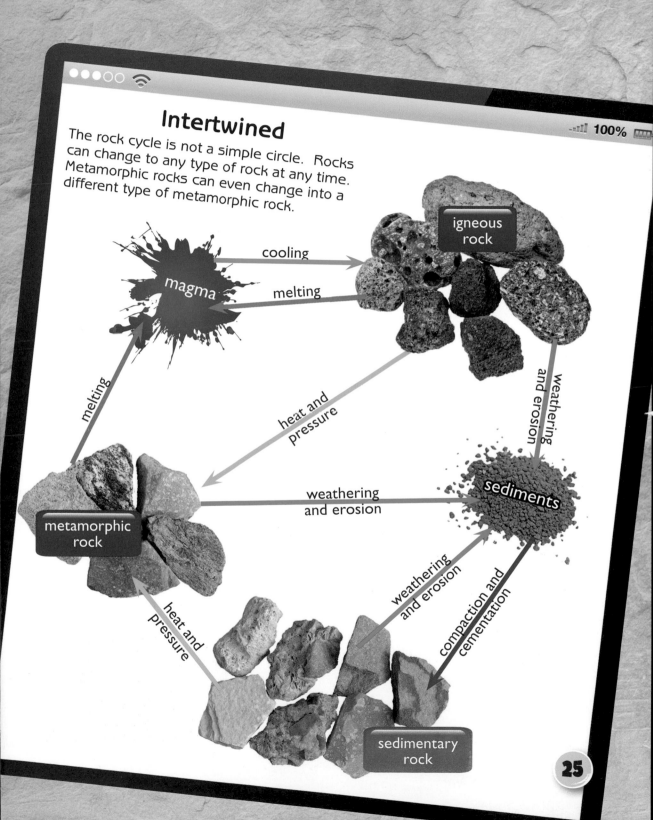

igneous rock

cooling

melting

magma

melting

weathering and erosion

heat and pressure

weathering and erosion

sediments

metamorphic rock

heat and pressure

weathering and erosion

compaction and cementation

sedimentary rock

Rocks are always on the move as they continually form, break down, and recycle. It takes weathering, heat, pressure, and erosion to make these changes happen. And, it takes millions of years for most of this to occur.

Rocks can form at any point in the rock cycle. Perhaps it's more accurate to look at these rock changes as a chain of events. With enough heat and pressure, igneous rock can turn into metamorphic rock. If sedimentary rocks are buried deep enough, they can change to metamorphic rock with a little heat. And if melted, sedimentary rock can change into igneous rock. The conditions have to be just right to set off these changes.

sedimentary rock

The next time you see rock, look a little closer. Look to see if there are sediments in the rock. Look at where you found it. Did it come from underground? Are crystals visible? Can you detect layers in the rock? Think about just how old that rock might be. Then, consider the journey that rock has taken up to this point and where it might end up in the future. Even rocks have a story. Understanding their story and the neverending journey they make gives us one more reason to stand in rock-solid awe of the ever-changing planet we call home.

Think Like a Scientist

How does a rock change throughout the rock cycle? Experiment and find out!

What to Get

- cheese grater
- crayons
- hot plate
- ice cube trays
- paper and pencil
- small saucepan

What to Do

1. Create a chart similar to this one. Then, unwrap each crayon. Observe these "igneous rocks," and record your observations.

Igneous Rock	Sediment	Sedimentary Rock

2. Have an adult carefully grate the crayons into small shavings. Observe these "sediments," and record your observations.

3. Make a pile of crayon shavings. Press down on them for 60 seconds. Observe these "sedimentary rocks," and record your observations.

4. Have an adult pour the pile of crayons into a saucepan and place the pan on a hot plate. Stir them until they are completely melted.

5. Pour the melted crayons into ice cube trays. Let them cool.

6. Observe the crayons again. What type of rock do the crayons represent now? What type of rock is not represented? How would the crayons change to represent that rock?

Glossary

crystals—small pieces of a substance that have many sides and are formed when the substance turns into a solid

dense—tightly compacted

erosion—movement of weathered rock and sediment

lithification—the process of sediments compacting and cementing to form solid rock

magma—hot, liquid rock below Earth's surface

metamorphism—a change in the makeup of a rock that is caused by pressure and heat

minerals—substances such as quartz and salt that are naturally formed underground

peat—dark material made of decaying plants that is burned for heat or added to garden soil

regional metamorphism—metamorphic rocks that are made within a large area through the movement of plates

sediments—very small pieces of rock, such as sand, gravel, and dust

strata—sheetlike mass of sedimentary rock or earth of one kind lying between beds of other kinds

tectonic plates—giant pieces of Earth's crust that move

volcanic bomb—chunk of igneous rock formed in the air from hardened lava

weathering—the slow breakdown of rock and sediment

Index

Your Turn!

Rock Collection

Start your own rock collection by first finding rocks around your home. Carefully observe the rocks. Choose rocks that you think are interesting or unique. Do research to determine the types of rocks you found. Label and display the rocks for all to enjoy!